OTTERS
TOOL USERS

KATIE
LAJINESS

AWESOME ANIMAL
POWERS

Big Buddy Books

An Imprint of Abdo Publishing
abdopublishing.com

abdopublishing.com

Published by Abdo Publishing, a division of ABDO, PO Box 398166, Minneapolis, Minnesota 55439.
Copyright © 2019 by Abdo Consulting Group, Inc. International copyrights reserved in all countries.
No part of this book may be reproduced in any form without written permission from the publisher.
Big Buddy Books™ is a trademark and logo of Abdo Publishing.

Printed in the United States of America, North Mankato, Minnesota.
052018
092018

Cover Photo: Cloudtail_the_Snow_Leopard/Getty Images.
Interior Photos: Alan Vernon/Getty Images (p. 11); Alex Wong/Getty Images News (p. 15); Cameron
    Rutt/Getty Images (p. 5); Dean Purcell/Getty Images News (p. 27); Erin Donalson/Getty Images
    (p. 19); GlobalP/Getty Images (pp. 7, 30); kwiktor/Getty Images (p. 17); matt6t6/Getty Images
    (p. 9); Nancy G Stock Photography, Greifenhagen/Alamy Stock Photo (p. 25); Oli Scarff/Getty
    Images News (p. 29); skibreck/Getty Images (p. 23); wellsie82/Getty Images (p. 21).

Coordinating Series Editor: Tamara L. Britton
Contributing Editor: Jill Roesler
Graphic Design: Jenny Christensen, Erika Weldon

Library of Congress Control Number: 2017961383

Publisher's Cataloging-in-Publication Data

Names: Lajiness, Katie, author.
Title: Otters: Tool users / by Katie Lajiness.
Other titles: Tool users
Description: Minneapolis, Minnesota : Abdo Publishing, 2019. | Series: Awesome animal
    powers | Includes online resources and index.
Identifiers: ISBN 9781532115028 (lib.bdg.) | ISBN 9781532155741 (ebook)
Subjects: LCSH: Otters--Juvenile literature. | Otters--Behavior--Juvenile literature. | Tool
    use in animals--Juvenile literature.
Classification: DDC 599.769--dc23

CONTENTS

THE OTTER

The world is full of awesome, powerful animals. Otters (AH-tuhrs) live in Africa, Asia, Europe, North America, and South America. They are some of the only **mammals** to use tools. Otters use rocks to break open shells underwater.

Sea otters are one of 13 types of otters. They are related to minks, badgers, and weasels.

BOLD BODIES

Male and female otters look the same. All have flat heads, whiskers, and small ears.

Otters have an undercoat and an outer coat that never shed. Their coats are the thickest on earth. Otters can be all different shades of brown. The fur on their bellies is a lighter color than the rest of their bodies.

DID YOU KNOW?

Otters can grow to weigh 75 pounds (34 kg).

Ears

Nose

Tail

Hidden Pouch

Webbed Feet

THAT'S AWESOME!

Otters are very smart. They are one of few animals to use tools like humans do. Otters can make tools out of rocks, wood, and empty shells.

These **mammals** have a pouch of loose skin under their front arm. This is where they store their favorite rock for opening shells.

In 2017, scientists discovered that otters have been using tools for millions of years.

Otters learned to use tools to make hunting and eating easier. They use rocks to knock shellfish loose from the sea floor. Then, they hammer the rock against the shell until it cracks open.

DID YOU KNOW?

While they spend most of their time in water, otters cannot breathe underwater.

Animals such as crows and monkeys have been trained to use tools. But otters use tools without any training.

WHERE IN THE

The different types of otters live in different areas around the world. The only **continent** on which they are not found is Australia.

Otters build **lodges** near the water. To construct these lodges, they will dig underground or gather branches and twigs into a nest.

WORLD?

■ = WHERE OTTERS LIVE

ARCTIC OCEAN

North America

Europe

Asia

PACIFIC OCEAN

NORTH ATLANTIC OCEAN

Africa

PACIFIC OCEAN

South America

INDIAN OCEAN

Australia

SOUTH ATLANTIC OCEAN

N
W E
S

DAILY LIFE

Otters can dive 300 feet (91 m) deep. They push themselves through the water using their strong legs and tails. On land, otters can run up to 29 miles (47 km) per hour.

Most of their time is spent underwater, swimming through **kelp** and seaweed. Sea otters wrap themselves in kelp to help them stay afloat. They are able to eat, sleep, and play this way.

Otters chirp, click, growl, and whistle to each other.

Otters swim by using their webbed back feet to push through the water. Their wide tails help them steer. These act like fins that allow otters to swim quickly. As they hunt, otters use their sharp claws to catch **prey**.

Otters can stay underwater for eight minutes. They close their nose and ears to keep water out while swimming.

AN OTTER'S LIFE

To relax, otters float on their backs. They float together in groups called rafts. A raft includes about 30 otters. They float together so they do not get lonely!

When sleeping in the water, otters hold hands with each other. This is so they do not drift apart.

Otters spend a lot of time **grooming** themselves. They blow air into their fur to keep warm.

An otter's fur is thick and **waterproof**. This helps keep otters warm when they swim in cool water.

Some types of otters eat up to 30 percent of their own body weight each day.

FAVORITE FOODS

These **mammals** often swim to find food. They hunt animals such as fish, clams, snails, and frogs. Adult sea otters must eat about 20 pounds (10 kg) of food each day!

Otters also eat crayfish, crabs, squid, sea urchins, and mussels.

BIRTH

Otters can **breed** when they are two or three years old. Female otters breed once or twice a year. Otter mothers give birth in their den or in the water. Most have one baby called a kit.

A mother can spend up to eight hours a day feeding her young. Before the mother dives for food, she wraps her kit in **kelp**.

These moms play with their kits. And they teach the kits to protect themselves.

A newborn otter weighs about four pounds (2 kg).

DEVELOPMENT

Most kits can live without their mothers when they are six to 12 months old. At a year old, kits can catch thier own shellfish and use rocks as tools. In the wild, most otters live for ten to 20 years.

Otters love to sunbathe during the day. And they do most of their hunting at night.

FUTURE

Otters face many dangers. Water **pollution** hurts the otter's **habitats**. This pollution can cause illness and even death.

Five of the 13 different types of otters are **endangered**. That is why there are groups working hard to keep the otters safe and healthy.

DID YOU KNOW?

The number of sea otters went down the most in the early 1900s. That is because trappers hunted otters to trade their furs.

All humans can help save otters. They can do so by recycling and disposing of waste properly.

FAST FACTS

ANIMAL TYPE: Mammal

SIZE: Between 28 inches (71 cm) and six feet (2 m)

WEIGHT: Between two to 75 pounds (1 to 34 kg)

HABITAT: Close to the land in either fresh or salt water

DIET: Fish, clams, snails, and crabs

AWESOME ANIMAL POWER: Their ability to use rocks and other tools to crack open shells.

GLOSSARY

breed to produce animals by mating.

continent one of the great divisions of land on the globe—Africa, Antarctica, Asia, Australia, Europe, North America, or South America.

endangered in danger of dying out.

groom to clean and care for.

habitat a place where a living thing is naturally found.

kelp a large brown seaweed.

lodge a den or resting place of an animal.

mammal a member of a group of living beings. Mammals make milk to feed their babies and usually have hair or fur on their skin.

pollution human waste that dirties or harms air, water, or land.

prey an animal hunted or killed by a predator for food.

waterproof not allowing water to pass through.

ONLINE RESOURCES

Booklinks
NONFICTION NETWORK
FREE! ONLINE NONFICTION RESOURCES

To learn more about otters, visit **abdobooklinks.com**. These links are routinely monitored and updated to provide the most current information available.

INDEX